WITHDRAWN

RIVER FOREST PUBLIC LIBRARY
735 Lathrop Avenue
River Forest, Illinois 60305
708 / 366-5205

3/06

27

WELCOME TO THE U.S.A.
MICHIGAN

RIVER FOREST PUBLIC LIBRARY
735 LATHROP
RIVER F...

Written by Ann Heinrichs   Illustrated by Matt Kania
Content Adviser: Dr. Roger Rosentreter, Professor, Department
of History, Michigan State University, East Lansing, Michigan

The Child's World

Published in the United States of America by The Child's World®
PO Box 326 • Chanhassen, MN 55317-0326
800-599-READ • www.childsworld.com

Photo Credits
Cover: Getty Images/Stone/Andy Sacks; frontispiece: Photodisc.

Interior: Corbis: 21, 30 (James L. Amos), 34 (Layne Kennedy); Richard Cummins/
Corbis: 25, 26; Brian Ford/Holland Tulip Time Festival: 17; Thom Forester/Motown
Historical Museum: 29; Lowell Georgia/Corbis: 14, 18; Getty Images/The Image
Bank/Bob Stefko: 9; The Henry Ford: 22; Kellogg's Cereal City USA: 33; Debi
Kruizenga/Paradise Parties and Vintage Photos: 6; Library of Congress: 23;
Mackinac State Historic Parks: 13; Michigan Historical Museum: 10.

Acknowledgments
The Child's World®: Mary Berendes, Publishing Director

Editorial Directions, Inc.: E. Russell Primm, Editorial Director; Katie Marsico, Associate
Editor; Judith Shiffer, Assistant Editor; Matt Messbarger, Editorial Assistant; Susan
Hindman, Copy Editor; Melissa McDaniel, Proofreader; Kevin Cunningham, Peter
Garnham, Matt Messbarger, Olivia Nellums, Chris Simms, Molly Symmonds, Katherine
Trickle, Carl Stephen Wender, Fact Checkers; Tim Griffin/IndexServ, Indexer; Cian
Loughlin O'Day, Photo Researcher and Editor

The Design Lab: Kathleen Petelinsek, Design and art production

Copyright © 2006 by The Child's World®
All rights reserved. No part of this book may be reproduced or utilized in any form or by
any means without written permission from the publisher.

Library of Congress Cataloging-in-Publication Data
Heinrichs, Ann.
   Michigan / by Ann Heinrichs.
      p. cm. — (Welcome to the U.S.A)
   Includes index.
   ISBN 1-59296-377-3 (library bound : alk. paper) 1. Michigan—Juvenile literature.
I. Title. II. Series.
   F566.3.H45 2006
   977.4—dc22   2004026168

Ann Heinrichs is the author of more than 100 books for children and young adults. She has also enjoyed successful careers as a children's book editor and an advertising copywriter. Ann grew up in Fort Smith, Arkansas, and lives in Chicago, Illinois.

About the Author
Ann Heinrichs

Matt Kania loves maps and, as a kid, dreamed of making them. In school he studied geography and cartography, and today he makes maps for a living. Matt's favorite thing about drawing maps is learning about the places they represent. Many of the maps he has created can be found in books, magazines, videos, Web sites, and public places.

About the
Map Illustrator
Matt Kania

On the cover: **Want to see how cars are made? Tour the Chrysler Plant in Sterling Heights!**
On page one: **Don't forget to spend a day by beautiful Lake Michigan!**

OUR MICHIGAN TRIP

Michigan's Nicknames: The Wolverine State, the Great Lakes State, and the Water Wonderland

What a trip's in store for you! You're about to tour Michigan.

You'll go snowmobiling and saw a log. You'll travel deep underground into a mine. You'll watch cereal and trucks being made. You'll meet Henry Ford and the Supremes. You'll even meet Tony the Tiger!

So what do you say? Shall we hit the road? Then buckle up, and hang on tight. We're off!

WELCOME TO MICHIGAN

As you travel through Michigan, watch for all the interesting facts along the way.

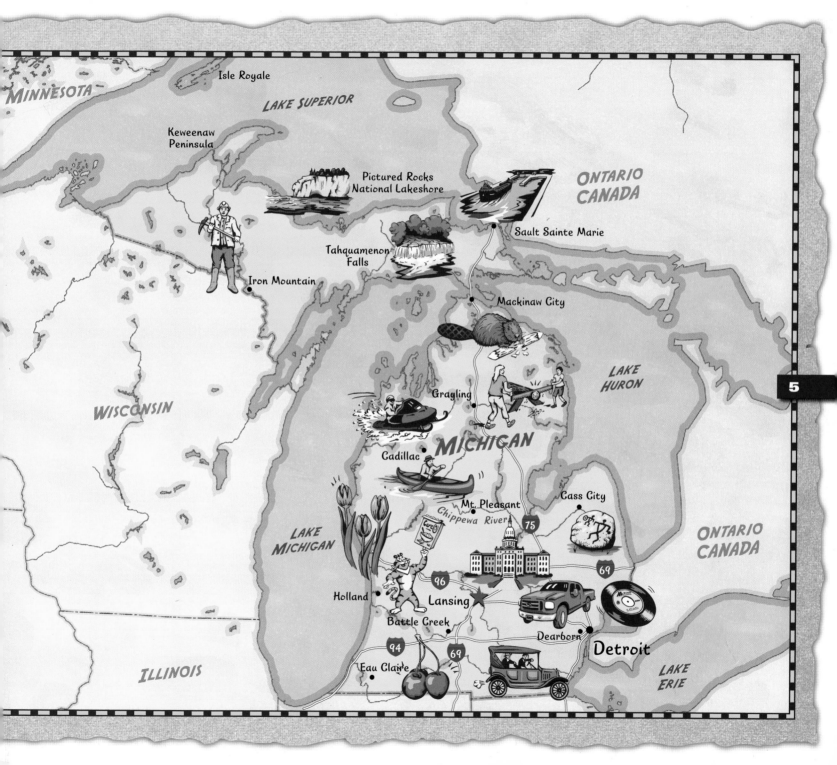

MINNESOTA

LAKE SUPERIOR

Isle Royale

Keweenaw
Peninsula

Pictured Rocks
National Lakeshore

ONTARIO
CANADA

Tahquamenon
Falls

Sault Sainte Marie

Iron Mountain

Mackinaw City

WISCONSIN

LAKE
HURON

Grayling

MICHIGAN

Cadillac

Mt. Pleasant

Cass City

Chippewa River

75

LAKE
MICHIGAN

Holland

96

Lansing

69

ONTARIO
CANADA

Battle Creek

Dearborn

Detroit

94

69

Eau Claire

LAKE
ERIE

ILLINOIS

Do you hear thunder? No, it's just water crashing over Tahquamenon Falls.

Pictured Rocks National Lakeshore is on Lake Superior. It has colorful and unusually shaped cliffs.

Tahquamenon Falls makes a roaring, thundering sound. Ojibwa Indians used to camp nearby. Later, the loggers came. They sent their logs tumbling down the waterfall.

Michigan has lots of waterfalls, rivers, and lakes. Four of the country's Great Lakes border Michigan. They are Lake Superior, Lake Michigan, Lake Huron, and Lake Erie.

Michigan has two main sections of land. In the north is the Upper **Peninsula.** That's where Tahquamenon Falls is. The Lower Peninsula is in the south. It's shaped like a mitten! The Upper and Lower Peninsulas don't touch each other. A narrow waterway runs between them. It's called the **Straits** of Mackinac.

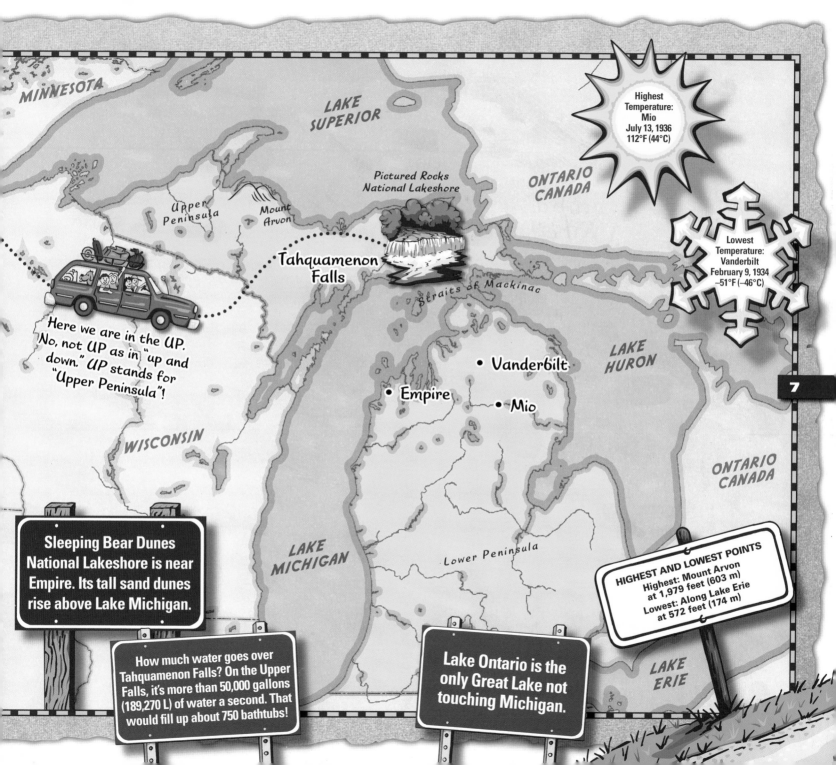

MINNESOTA

LAKE SUPERIOR

ONTARIO CANADA

Upper Peninsula

Mount Arvon

Pictured Rocks National Lakeshore

Tahquamenon Falls

Straits of Mackinac

Here we are in the UP. No, not UP as in "up and down." UP stands for "Upper Peninsula"!

Vanderbilt

Empire

Mio

LAKE HURON

ONTARIO CANADA

WISCONSIN

Lower Peninsula

LAKE MICHIGAN

Highest Temperature:
Mio
July 13, 1936
112°F (44°C)

Lowest Temperature:
Vanderbilt
February 9, 1934
−51°F (−46°C)

Sleeping Bear Dunes National Lakeshore is near Empire. Its tall sand dunes rise above Lake Michigan.

How much water goes over Tahquamenon Falls? On the Upper Falls, it's more than 50,000 gallons (189,270 L) of water a second. That would fill up about 750 bathtubs!

Lake Ontario is the only Great Lake not touching Michigan.

HIGHEST AND LOWEST POINTS
Highest: Mount Arvon at 1,979 feet (603 m)
Lowest: Along Lake Erie at 572 feet (174 m)

LAKE ERIE

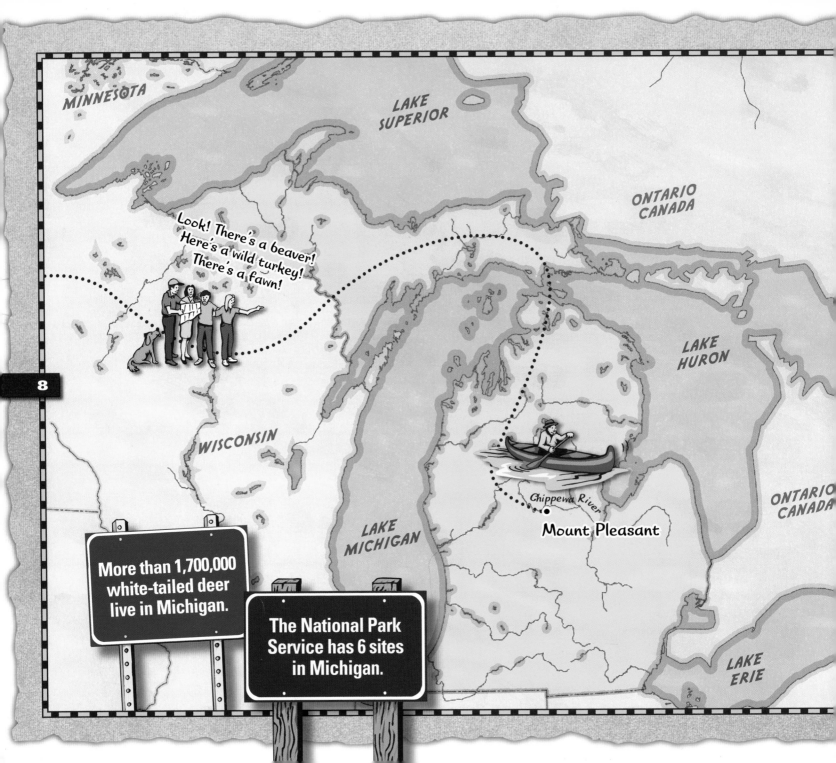

A blue heron marches through the grass. These graceful birds call Michigan home.

Have you ever watched wildlife from a canoe? The Chippewa River is great for viewing wildlife. And Mount Pleasant is a perfect place to start. Just launch your canoe from the nature park there. Soon you'll be drifting along the river's shady banks.

You'll see deer with their new fawns. You might also spot wild turkeys nearby. If it's very quiet, you'll see beavers, too. Blue herons are along the banks. Hawks and eagles soar high in the sky.

Forests cover more than half of Michigan. The state also has thousands of rivers and streams. That's why it's called the Water Wonderland.

STATE FLOWER
APPLE BLOSSOM

STATE TREE
WHITE PINE

STATE BIRD
AMERICAN ROBIN

9

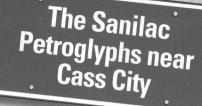
Imagine carving an entire picture onto a stone. That wouldn't be easy to do!

You'll see dozens of stone carvings near Cass City. They're called the Sanilac Petroglyphs. Petroglyphs are pictures carved in stone.

American Indians carved these pictures. They created this artwork hundreds of years ago. No one knows much about the artists, though.

Thousands of American Indians once lived in Michigan. White people arrived in the 1660s. They were French explorers from Canada. At that time, Canada was a **colony** of France. French trappers and traders soon arrived. Roman Catholic priests came, too. They hoped to **convert** the American Indians to Christianity.

10

Visitors prepare to tour the Sanilac Petroglyphs.

The Sanilac Petroglyphs include a picture of a water panther. This mythical animal was honored by American Indians.

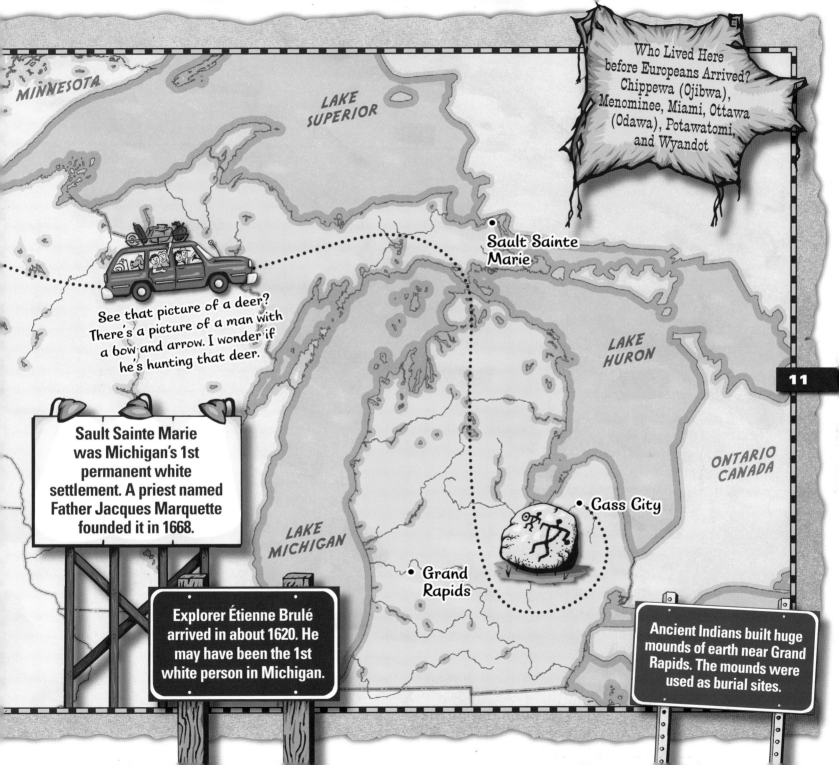

MINNESOTA

LAKE SUPERIOR

Who Lived Here before Europeans Arrived? Chippewa (Ojibwa), Menominee, Miami, Ottawa (Odawa), Potawatomi, and Wyandot

Sault Sainte Marie

LAKE HURON

See that picture of a deer? There's a picture of a man with a bow and arrow. I wonder if he's hunting that deer.

Sault Sainte Marie was Michigan's 1st permanent white settlement. A priest named Father Jacques Marquette founded it in 1668.

LAKE MICHIGAN

ONTARIO CANADA

Cass City

Grand Rapids

Explorer Étienne Brulé arrived in about 1620. He may have been the 1st white person in Michigan.

Ancient Indians built huge mounds of earth near Grand Rapids. The mounds were used as burial sites.

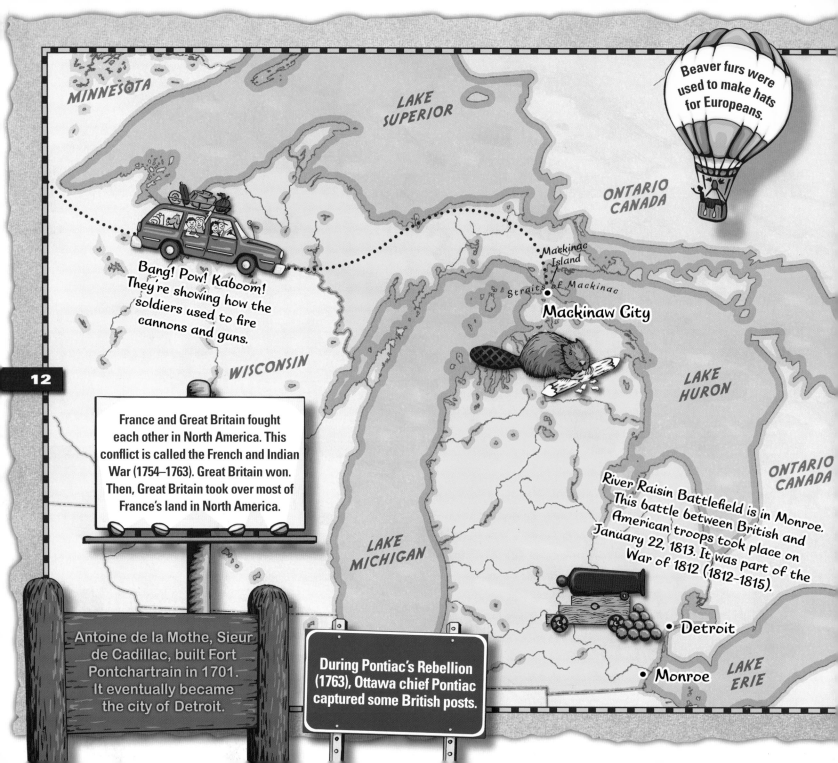

Beaver furs were used to make hats for Europeans.

MINNESOTA

LAKE SUPERIOR

ONTARIO CANADA

Bang! Pow! Kaboom! They're showing how the soldiers used to fire cannons and guns.

Mackinac Island

Straits of Mackinac

Mackinaw City

WISCONSIN

LAKE HURON

France and Great Britain fought each other in North America. This conflict is called the French and Indian War (1754–1763). Great Britain won. Then, Great Britain took over most of France's land in North America.

ONTARIO CANADA

River Raisin Battlefield is in Monroe. This battle between British and American troops took place on January 22, 1813. It was part of the War of 1812 (1812–1815).

LAKE MICHIGAN

Antoine de la Mothe, Sieur de Cadillac, built Fort Pontchartrain in 1701. It eventually became the city of Detroit.

During Pontiac's Rebellion (1763), Ottawa chief Pontiac captured some British posts.

• Detroit

• Monroe

LAKE ERIE

What's for dinner? This Native American woman cooks fish at Michilimackinac.

A fur trader counts his animal skins. A soldier stands guard nearby. A woman cooks dinner over an open fire. You'll see them all at Colonial Michilimackinac.

Michilimackinac was a fur-trading post and army fort. French traders built it in 1715. Furs were a big business in this region. The forests were full of furry animals. Both the French and the Indians trapped them. They traded animal skins at the trading posts.

Great Britain won Michigan from France in 1763. After that, Michilimackinac became a British fort. Michigan soon changed hands again. Americans beat the British in the Revolutionary War (1775–1783). Then Michigan became part of the United States.

Historic Fort Mackinac is on Mackinac Island in the Straits of Mackinac. British soldiers built it in the late 1700s.

The Big John sign welcomes tourists to Iron Mountain.

14

The Library of Michigan opened in Detroit in 1828.

Put on your hard hat. Then hop aboard the train. You're heading deep underground. How deep? Four hundred feet (120 meters)! You're touring an iron mine at Iron Mountain. You'll see how miners used to work down there. They wore hard hats, too.

The Upper Peninsula is rich in iron **ore.** People began mining there in the 1840s. Copper was discovered there at about the same time. Thousands of people rushed in for mining jobs.

All over Michigan, **pioneers** were making new homes. Many were **immigrants** from European lands. Everyone was looking for a better life.

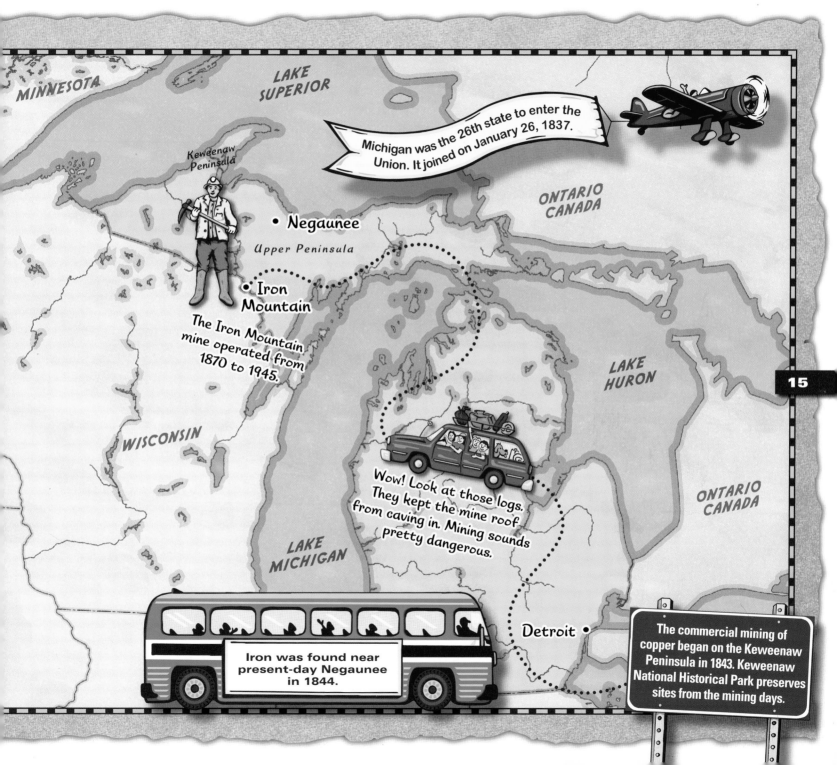

MINNESOTA

LAKE SUPERIOR

Keweenaw Peninsula

Michigan was the 26th state to enter the Union. It joined on January 26, 1837.

ONTARIO CANADA

• Negaunee

Upper Peninsula

• Iron Mountain

The Iron Mountain mine operated from 1870 to 1945.

LAKE HURON

WISCONSIN

15

Wow! Look at those logs. They kept the mine roof from caving in. Mining sounds pretty dangerous.

ONTARIO CANADA

LAKE MICHIGAN

Detroit •

Iron was found near present-day Negaunee in 1844.

The commercial mining of copper began on the Keweenaw Peninsula in 1843. Keweenaw National Historical Park preserves sites from the mining days.

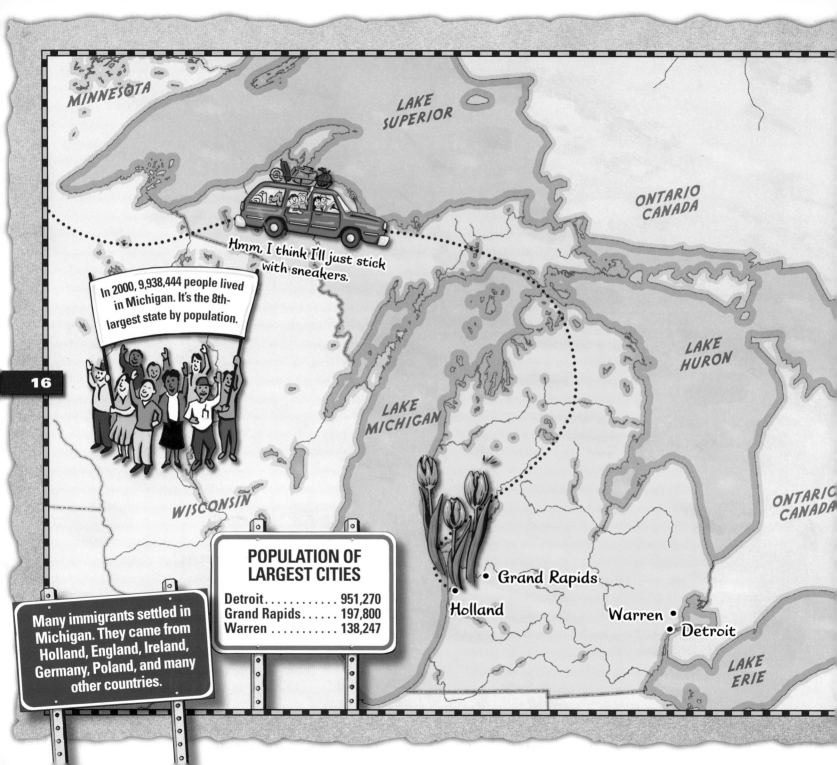

MINNESOTA

LAKE SUPERIOR

ONTARIO CANADA

Hmm, I think I'll just stick with sneakers.

In 2000, 9,938,444 people lived in Michigan. It's the 8th-largest state by population.

LAKE HURON

LAKE MICHIGAN

WISCONSIN

ONTARIO CANADA

POPULATION OF LARGEST CITIES

Detroit............951,270
Grand Rapids......197,800
Warren...........138,247

Many immigrants settled in Michigan. They came from Holland, England, Ireland, Germany, Poland, and many other countries.

• Grand Rapids

• Holland

Warren •
• Detroit

LAKE ERIE

The Tulip Time Festival in Holland

It's Holland's Tulip Time Festival! Want to march in the parade? Don't forget your wooden shoes!

Clack, clack, thunk! Those dancers sure make a lot of noise. But that's not surprising—they're wearing wooden shoes!

It's the Tulip Time Festival in Holland. Lots of people are wearing **traditional** Dutch costumes. That includes *klompen,* or wooden shoes.

A group of immigrants settled here in 1847. Most were Dutch people. They came from the Netherlands. This country is often called Holland. The immigrants named Holland, Michigan, after their homeland. The Dutch are famous for their tulips. So the townspeople of Holland began planting them. They bloom during the festival.

Visitors enjoy a boat tour of the Soo Locks.

Your boat glides through a gate. The gate shuts and locks tight. Another gate opens, and water rushes in. The water lifts your boat two stories higher. Then you sail into Lake Superior.

You're touring the Soo Locks. They solved a big problem in the 1800s. Iron and other goods were produced along Lake Superior. But how could people ship those goods?

The Saint Mary's River seemed like a good route. It flows from Lake Superior to Lake Huron. From there, boats could travel far and wide. But the river had a big waterfall. People dug a **canal** around the falls. They built locks to raise and lower water levels. Then boats could move up and down!

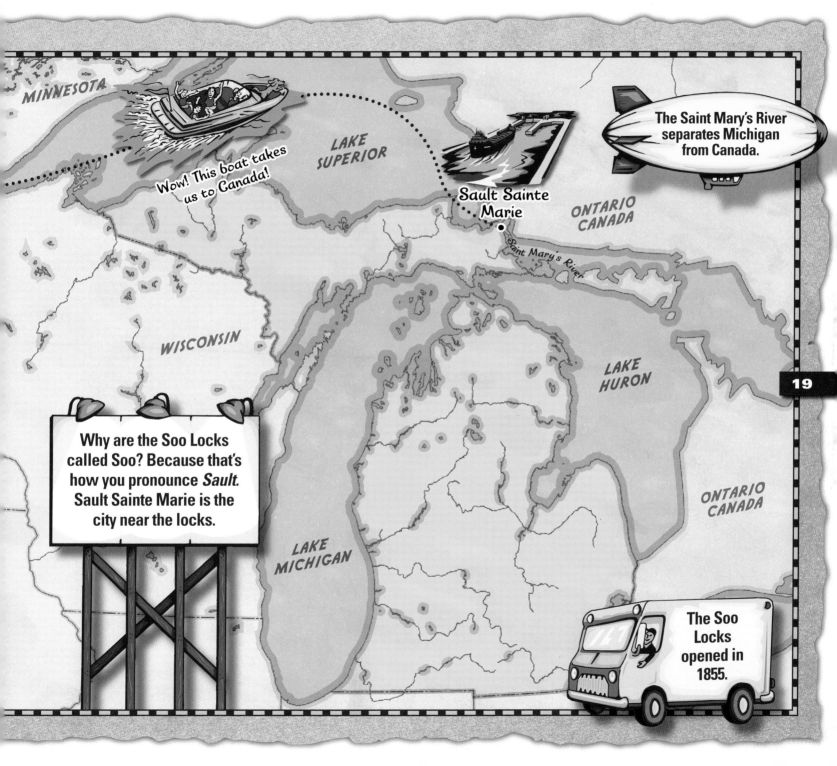

Wow! This boat takes us to Canada!

MINNESOTA

LAKE SUPERIOR

Sault Sainte Marie

The Saint Mary's River separates Michigan from Canada.

ONTARIO CANADA

Saint Mary's River

WISCONSIN

LAKE HURON

19

LAKE MICHIGAN

ONTARIO CANADA

Why are the Soo Locks called Soo? Because that's how you pronounce *Sault*. Sault Sainte Marie is the city near the locks.

The Soo Locks opened in 1855.

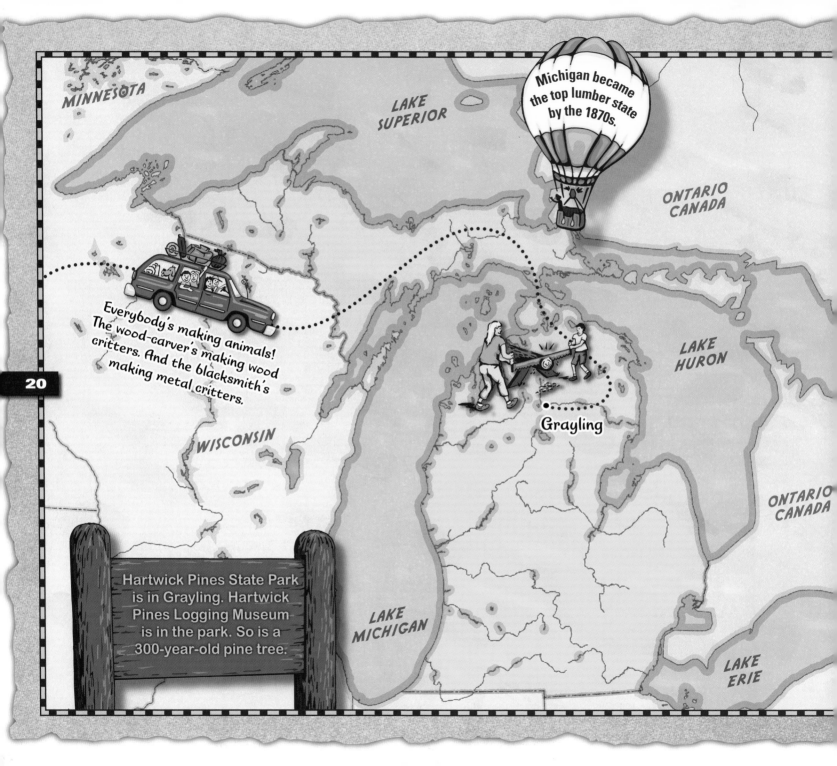

MINNESOTA

LAKE SUPERIOR

ONTARIO CANADA

Michigan became the top lumber state by the 1870s.

Everybody's making animals! The wood-carver's making wood critters. And the blacksmith's making metal critters.

WISCONSIN

Grayling

LAKE HURON

Hartwick Pines State Park is in Grayling. Hartwick Pines Logging Museum is in the park. So is a 300-year-old pine tree.

LAKE MICHIGAN

ONTARIO CANADA

LAKE ERIE

Wood Shaving Days at Hartwick Pines

Logging sure was hard work! These men logged in Michigan in the late 1800s.

Have you ever seen a two-person saw? It's long, with handles on both ends. One person grabs each handle. Then they lean back and forth to saw. That's how people used to saw logs.

You can try it yourself at Wood Shaving Days. This festival celebrates Michigan's logging days. You'll see wood-carvers and blacksmiths. There's a steam-powered sawmill, too.

Logging became a big **industry** in the late 1800s. Loggers lived in logging camps. They cut down trees and sawed huge logs. Then they floated the logs down a river. The logs arrived at a sawmill. There they were sawed into flat boards. People built homes and stores with this wood.

Things are really noisy here. Machines are lifting, screwing, and drilling. And look what comes out at the end—a truck!

You're touring the Ford Rouge Factory. Henry Ford opened it in 1917. He was a pioneer in making cars.

People used to travel in horse-drawn carriages. But Ford began thinking about a "horseless carriage." He started the Ford Motor Company in 1903. His Model T cars became super popular. Many car factories opened in southeastern Michigan. Detroit became the nation's car-making center.

Want to see some cool old-time cars? Just head to the Ford Rouge Factory!

Detroit is called the Motor City. Some people just call it Motown!

How did the Ford Rouge Factory get its name? It's on the banks of the Rouge River! *Rouge* is French for "red."

22

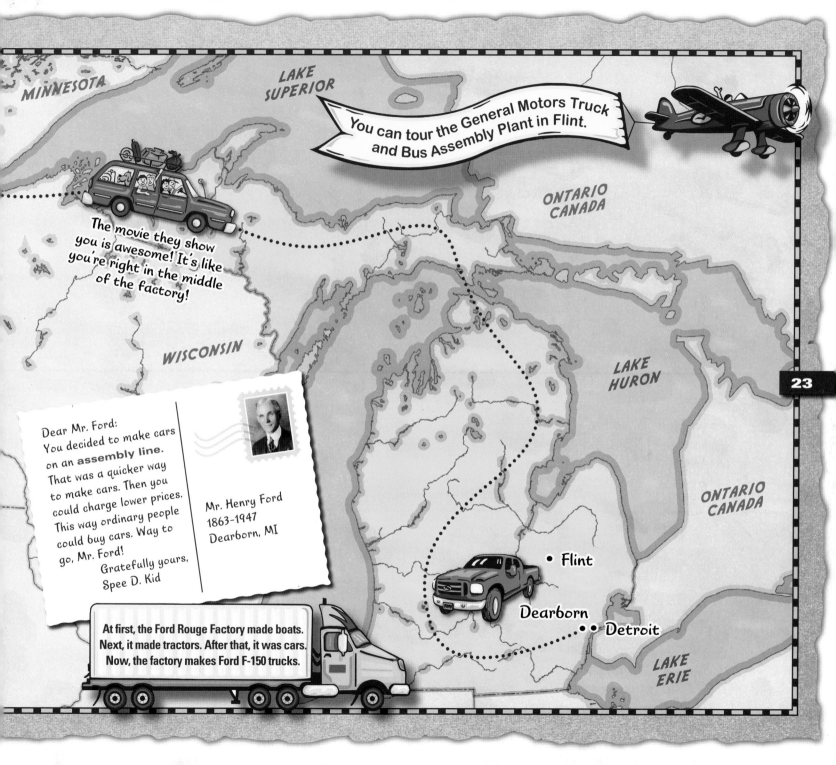

MINNESOTA

LAKE SUPERIOR

You can tour the General Motors Truck and Bus Assembly Plant in Flint.

ONTARIO CANADA

The movie they show you is awesome! It's like you're right in the middle of the factory!

WISCONSIN

LAKE HURON

Dear Mr. Ford:
You decided to make cars on an **assembly line**. That was a quicker way to make cars. Then you could charge lower prices. This way ordinary people could buy cars. Way to go, Mr. Ford!
Gratefully yours,
Spee D. Kid

Mr. Henry Ford
1863-1947
Dearborn, MI

ONTARIO CANADA

• Flint

Dearborn
• • Detroit

At first, the Ford Rouge Factory made boats. Next, it made tractors. After that, it was cars. Now, the factory makes Ford F-150 trucks.

LAKE ERIE

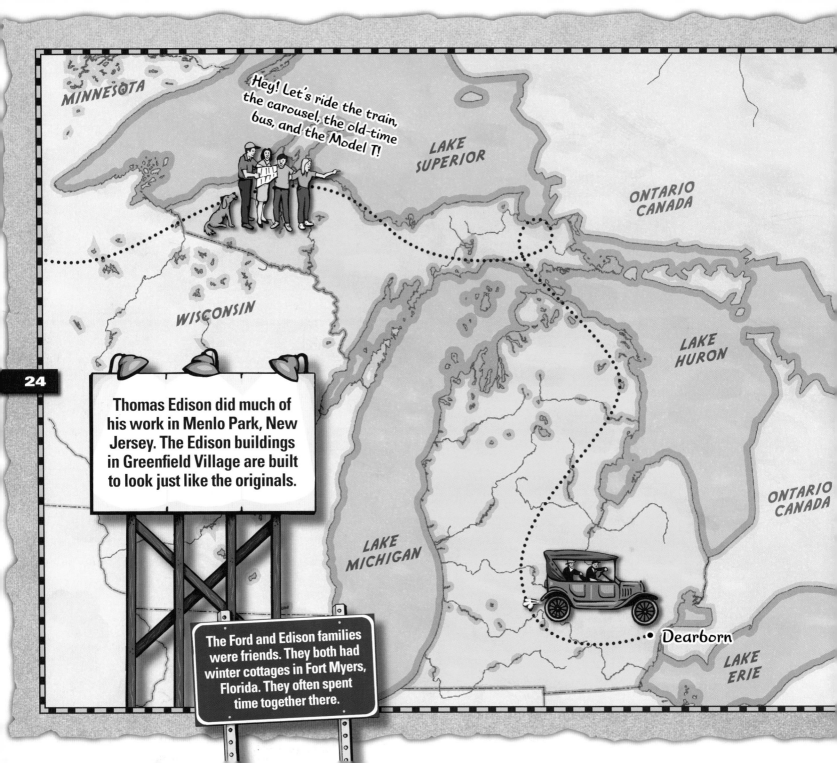

24

Hey! Let's ride the train, the carousel, the old-time bus, and the Model T!

Thomas Edison did much of his work in Menlo Park, New Jersey. The Edison buildings in Greenfield Village are built to look just like the originals.

The Ford and Edison families were friends. They both had winter cottages in Fort Myers, Florida. They often spent time together there.

Dearborn

MINNESOTA

LAKE SUPERIOR

ONTARIO CANADA

WISCONSIN

LAKE HURON

LAKE MICHIGAN

ONTARIO CANADA

LAKE ERIE

Greenfield Village in Dearborn

Chug along in a Ford Model T. Hop aboard a paddle-wheel steamboat. Ride a horse-drawn carriage through town. You're in Greenfield Village!

This village spreads out over many acres. It gives you a feel for the past. Farm families are doing their chores. People are making things they need by hand.

One area focuses on Thomas Edison. He invented lightbulbs and many other things. You'll explore his workshop and see his inventions.

Nearby is the Henry Ford Museum. You'll see thousands of machines and everyday items there. They range from airplanes and cars to toasters!

Vroom! Check out this race car at the Henry Ford Museum.

25

The Henry Ford Museum's IMAX theater is 6 stories high!

The State Capitol
in Lansing

Look up! You're staring at the dome in Michigan's capitol.

Welcome to Lansing, the capital of Michigan!

The State Capitol in Lansing

Touring the state capitol is quite a trip. Just walk in and look down. You're walking on a floor made of glass! It seems to sink down like a bowl. But that's just a trick on your eyes. The floor is perfectly flat.

This building houses many state government offices. The state government has three branches. Michigan's governor heads one branch. This branch sees that laws are carried out. Another branch makes laws for the state. Judges make up the third branch. They listen to cases in courts. They decide whether someone has broken the law.

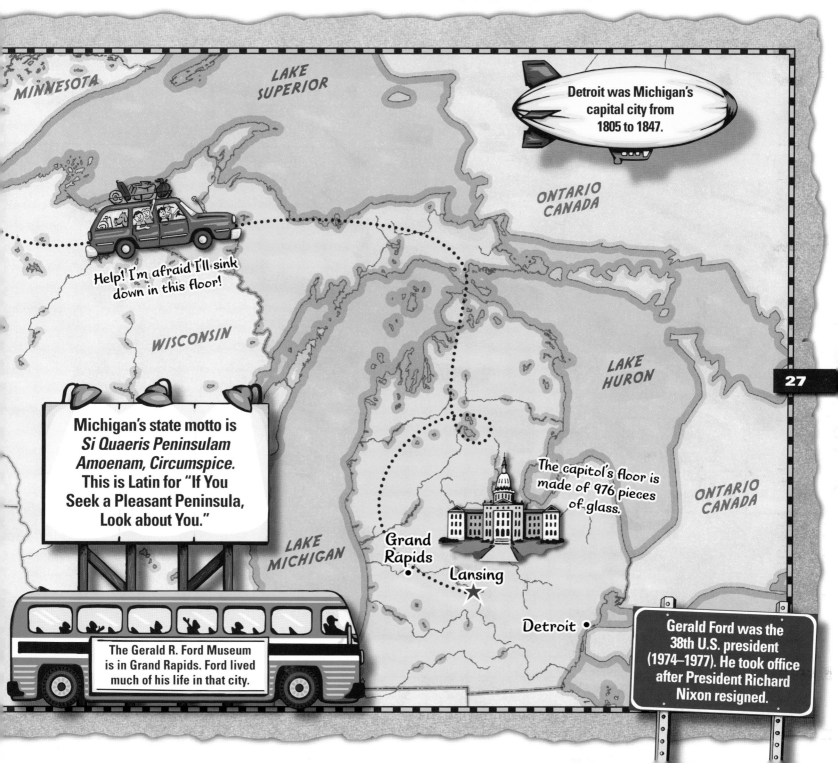

MINNESOTA

LAKE SUPERIOR

Detroit was Michigan's capital city from 1805 to 1847.

ONTARIO CANADA

Help! I'm afraid I'll sink down in this floor!

WISCONSIN

LAKE HURON

Michigan's state motto is *Si Quaeris Peninsulam Amoenam, Circumspice.* This is Latin for "If You Seek a Pleasant Peninsula, Look about You."

The capitol's floor is made of 976 pieces of glass.

ONTARIO CANADA

LAKE MICHIGAN

Grand Rapids

Lansing ★

Detroit •

The Gerald R. Ford Museum is in Grand Rapids. Ford lived much of his life in that city.

Gerald Ford was the 38th U.S. president (1974–1977). He took office after President Richard Nixon resigned.

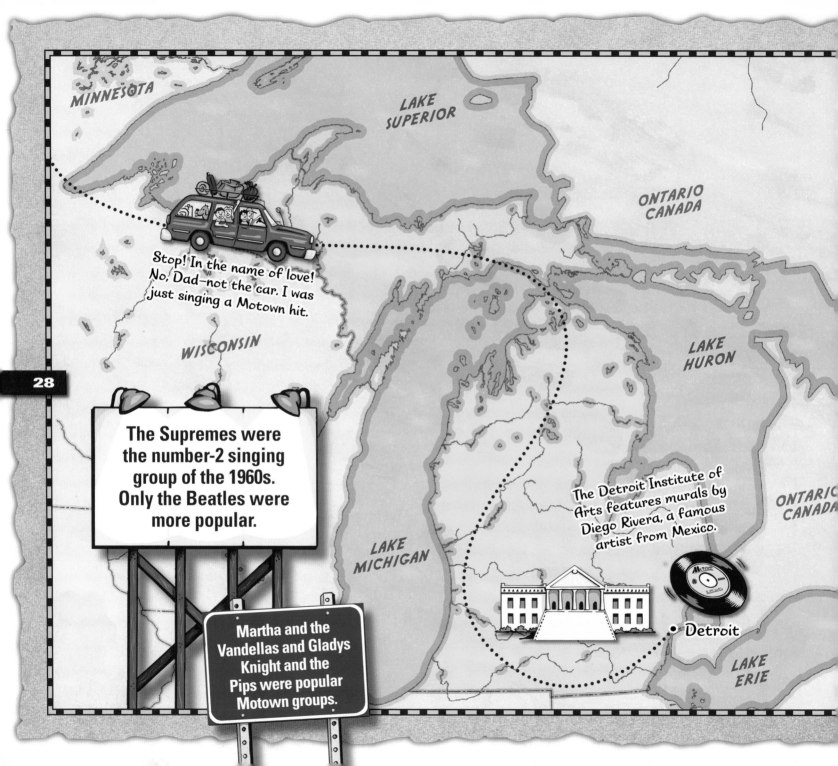

Stop! In the name of love! No, Dad—not the car. I was just singing a Motown hit.

The Supremes were the number-2 singing group of the 1960s. Only the Beatles were more popular.

Martha and the Vandellas and Gladys Knight and the Pips were popular Motown groups.

The Detroit Institute of Arts features murals by Diego Rivera, a famous artist from Mexico.

Detroit

Motown Music and Detroit's Motown Museum

Remember that city called Motown? It's Detroit, the Motor City. But Detroit is famous for more than cars. It's where Motown music was born!

Motown music began in the 1960s. It's an African American music style. It combines gospel, soul, and rhythm and blues. Smokey Robinson and the Miracles were big Motown stars. So were the Supremes and the Temptations.

People all over the country loved Motown music. Black musicians had never been this popular before. Motown opened the door for many other black musicians. Want to learn all about Motown and its stars? Visit the Motown Museum in Detroit!

Are you a fan of Motown music? Be sure to visit the Motown Museum in Detroit.

Stevie Wonder was a Motown star even as a child. He recorded his 1st song at age 12.

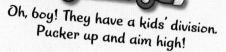

Oh, boy! They have a kids' division. Pucker up and aim high!

30

A Michigan farmer harvests cherries in Traverse City.

Thwit! Thwit! Thwit! Stand back. It's the International Cherry Pit Spitting Championship!

This may seem like a silly contest. But the spitters are very serious. They get three chances to spit. What if they swallow a cherry pit? Then they lose that turn!

Michigan is a leading state in growing cherries. Its rich soil is good for raising many crops. Corn is the leading field crop. Farmers also grow wheat, hay, and soybeans.

Many Michigan farmers raise flowers and shrubs. One Michigan crop is very popular in December. It's Christmas trees!

Only Oregon grows more Christmas trees than Michigan.

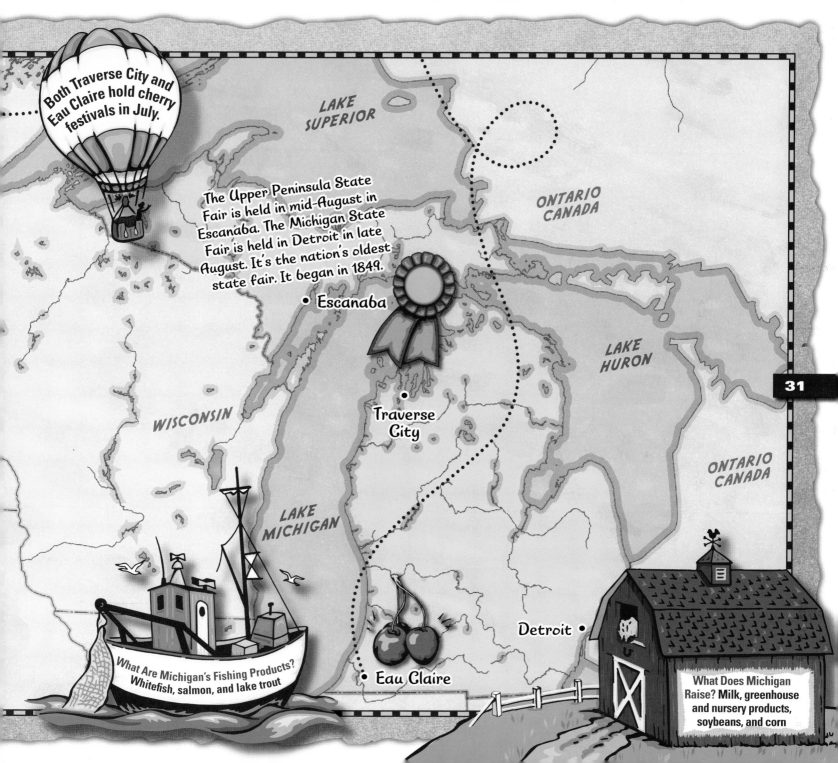

Both Traverse City and Eau Claire hold cherry festivals in July.

The Upper Peninsula State Fair is held in mid-August in Escanaba. The Michigan State Fair is held in Detroit in late August. It's the nation's oldest state fair. It began in 1849.

LAKE SUPERIOR

ONTARIO CANADA

• Escanaba

LAKE HURON

WISCONSIN

•
Traverse City

ONTARIO CANADA

LAKE MICHIGAN

What Are Michigan's Fishing Products? Whitefish, salmon, and lake trout

Detroit •

• Eau Claire

What Does Michigan Raise? Milk, greenhouse and nursery products, soybeans, and corn

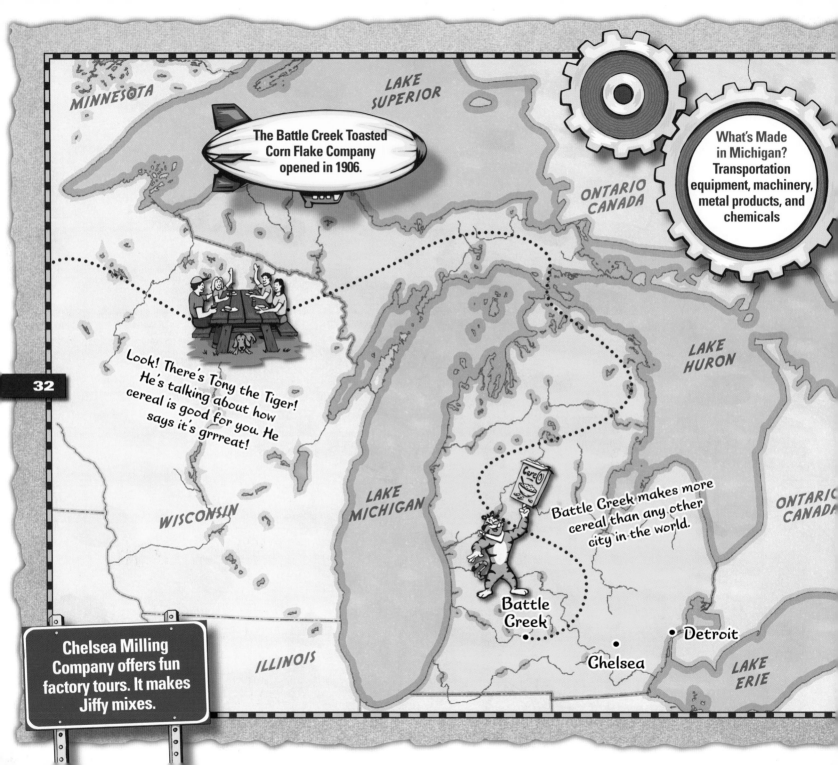

The Battle Creek Toasted Corn Flake Company opened in 1906.

What's Made in Michigan? Transportation equipment, machinery, metal products, and chemicals

Look! There's Tony the Tiger! He's talking about how cereal is good for you. He says it's grrreat!

Battle Creek makes more cereal than any other city in the world.

Chelsea Milling Company offers fun factory tours. It makes Jiffy mixes.

Y ou're looking at a big mixing tank. A railroad car dumps corn and flavorings in. Finally, there's the finished product—cornflakes!

This is your tour of Kellogg's Cereal City. You'll learn how breakfast cereal was born. And you'll see just how it's made. You even get a sample of cereal to take home with you!

Cereal is an important factory product in Michigan. Both Post and Kellogg's cereals got their start there. But don't forget Detroit, the Motor City! Cars are still Michigan's leading factory goods.

Want to learn more about your breakfast? Tour Kellogg's Cereal City!

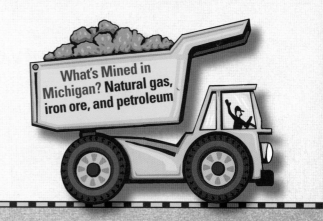

What's Mined in Michigan? Natural gas, iron ore, and petroleum

33

34

Swoosh! Snowmobilers enjoy the winter weather on Mackinac Island.

The Snowmobile Festival in Cadillac

The racers zoom through jumps, twists, and turns. Swoosh! They reach the finish line. You're watching the North American Snowmobile Festival. Want to try it yourself? No problem. They have kids' races, too.

Snowmobiling is a big sport in Michigan. People love snowmobiling through snowy forests. They whip around trees and rumble over logs. Snow skiing and ice skating are popular, too. When it's warmer, people enjoy hiking and camping. Some take canoes down the rivers. Others like fishing in the clear streams.

There's a lot to do along the lakeshores, too. You can climb sand dunes. Then sit down and slide to the bottom. Whee!

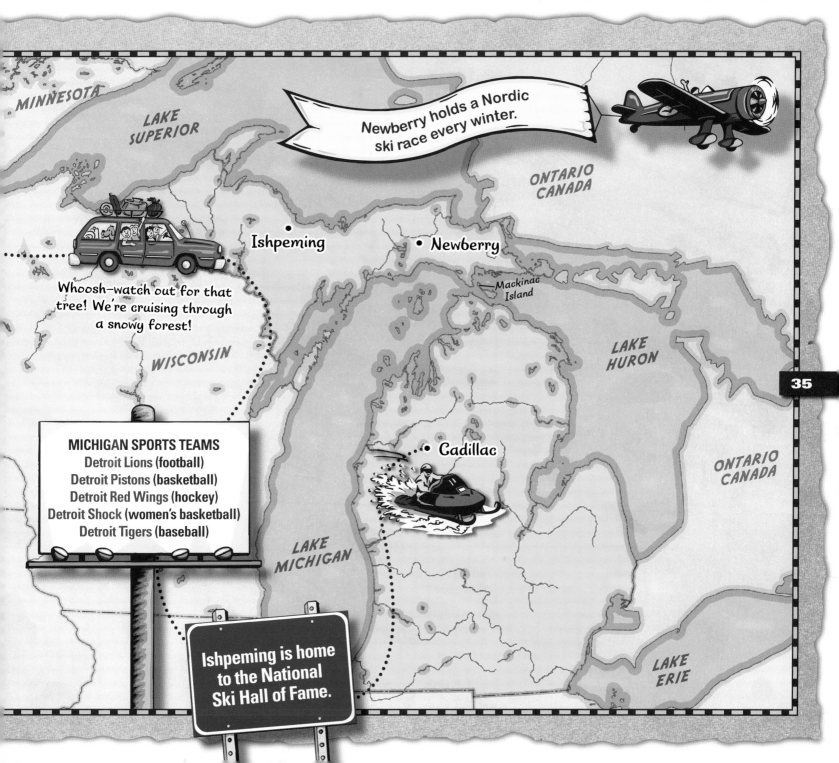

Newberry holds a Nordic ski race every winter.

MINNESOTA

LAKE SUPERIOR

ONTARIO CANADA

Ishpeming

• Newberry

Mackinac Island

Whoosh—watch out for that tree! We're cruising through a snowy forest!

WISCONSIN

LAKE HURON

ONTARIO CANADA

MICHIGAN SPORTS TEAMS
Detroit Lions (football)
Detroit Pistons (basketball)
Detroit Red Wings (hockey)
Detroit Shock (women's basketball)
Detroit Tigers (baseball)

• Cadillac

LAKE MICHIGAN

LAKE ERIE

Ishpeming is home to the National Ski Hall of Fame.

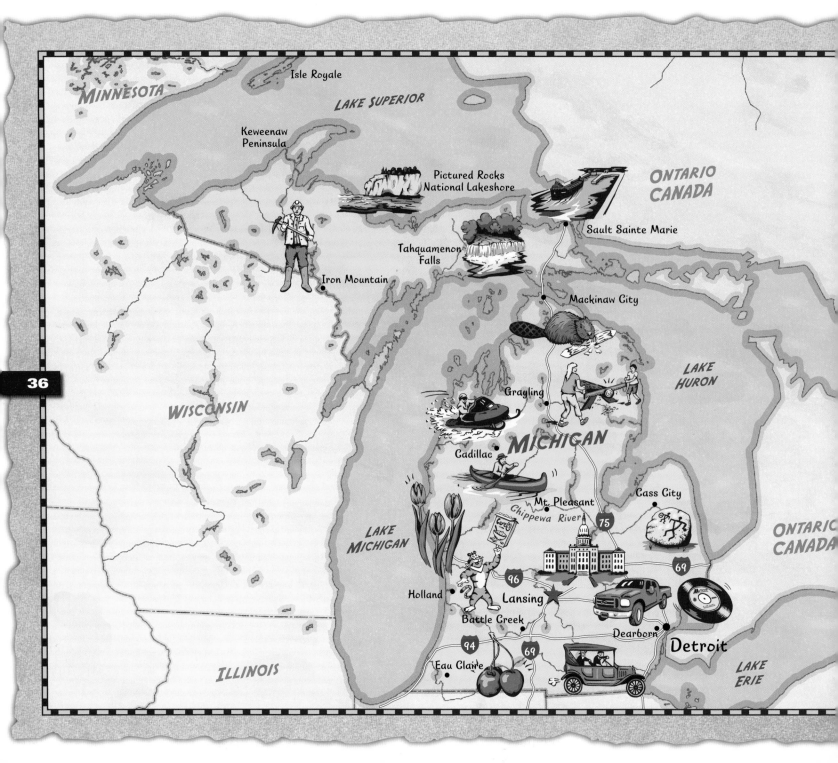

MINNESOTA

Isle Royale

LAKE SUPERIOR

Keweenaw
Peninsula

Pictured Rocks
National Lakeshore

ONTARIO
CANADA

Tahquamenon
Falls

Sault Sainte Marie

Iron Mountain

Mackinaw City

WISCONSIN

LAKE
HURON

Grayling

MICHIGAN

Cadillac

Cass City

Mt. Pleasant

Chippewa River

75

LAKE
MICHIGAN

ONTARIO
CANADA

96

69

Holland

Lansing

94

Battle Creek

Dearborn

Detroit

69

Eau Claire

LAKE
ERIE

ILLINOIS

OUR TRIP

We visited many amazing places on our trip! We also met a lot of interesting people along the way. Look at the map on the left. Use your finger to trace all the places we have been.

Where is Pictured Rocks National Lakeshore located? See page 6 for the answer.

How tall is Mount Arvon? Page 7 has the answer.

Who founded the city of Sault Sainte Marie? See page 11 for the answer.

How did the Ford Rouge Factory get its name? Look on page 22 for the answer.

What's made at the Ford Rouge Factory? Page 23 has the answer.

How tall is the Henry Ford Museum's IMAX theater? Turn to page 25 for the answer.

What was Michigan's capital from 1805 to 1847? Look on page 27 and find out!

Who is Diego Rivera? Turn to page 28 for the answer.

That was a great trip! We have traveled all over Michigan!
There are a few places that we didn't have time for, though. Next time, we plan to visit the Ambassador Bridge in Detroit. This bridge connects 2 countries. It stretches over the Detroit River between the United States and Windsor, Canada. It was built in 1929.

More Places to Visit in Michigan

WORDS TO KNOW

assembly line (uh-SEM-blee LINE) a line of workers and machines that repeat the same actions to produce a product

canal (kuh-NAL) a waterway dug by people

colony (KOL-uh-nee) a land with ties to a parent country

convert (kuhn-VURT) to change something such as a person's religion or beliefs

immigrants (IM-uh-gruhntz) people who move from their home country to a new land

industry (IN-duh-stree) a type of business

mythical (MITH-ih-kuhl) something that is made up or imaginary

ore (OR) rock that is filled with a metal

peninsula (puh-NIN-suh-luh) land almost completely surrounded by water

pioneers (pye-uh-NEERZ) people who move into a place where no one has settled before

straits (STRAYTZ) narrow waterways that connect 2 large bodies of water

traditional (truh-DISH-uhn-uhl) following long-held customs

Michigan covers 56,804 square miles (147,121 sq km). It's the 22nd-largest state in size.

STATE SYMBOLS

State bird: American robin

State fish: Brook trout

State flower: Apple blossom

State game mammal: White-tailed deer

State gem: Chlorastrolite

State reptile: Painted turtle

State soil: Kalkaska sand

State stone: Petoskey stone

State tree: White pine

State wildflower: Dwarf lake iris

State flag

State seal

STATE SONG

"Michigan, My Michigan"

For many years, people thought Michigan had no official state song. But recently, the Michigan Historical Center discovered "My Michigan," with words by Giles Kavanagh and music by H. O'Reilly Clint. "My Michigan" was made an official state song in 1937. But "Michigan, My Michigan" has long been considered the unofficial state song and is still the popular choice in patriotic programs throughout the state. Winifred Lee Brent wrote the 1st version in 1862. Douglas Malloch wrote new words in 1902. His version is used today.

A song to thee, fair State of mine,
Michigan, my Michigan;
But greater song than this is thine,
Michigan, my Michigan;
The whisper of the forest tree,
The thunder of the inland sea;
Unite in one grand symphony
Of Michigan, my Michigan.

I sing a State of all the best,
Michigan, my Michigan;
I sing a State with riches blest,
Michigan, my Michigan;
Thy mines unmask a hidden store,
But richer thy historic lore,
More great the love thy builders
  bore,
Oh, Michigan, my Michigan.

How fair the bosom of thy lakes,
Michigan, my Michigan;
What melody each river makes,
Michigan, my Michigan;
As to thy lakes the rivers tend,
Thy exiled children to thee send
Devotion that shall never end,
Oh, Michigan, my Michigan.

Thou rich in wealth that makes
  a State,
Michigan, my Michigan;
Thou great in things that make
  us great,
Michigan, my Michigan;
Our loyal voices sound they
  claim
Upon the golden roll of fame
Our loyal hands shall write the
  name
Of Michigan, my Michigan.

FAMOUS PEOPLE

Boeing, William E. (1881–1956), aircraft company founder

Coppola, Francis Ford (1939–), film director

Curtis, Christopher Paul (ca. 1954–), children's author

Ford, Gerald (1913–), 28th U.S. president

Ford, Henry (1863–1947), inventor, automobile manufacturer

Franklin, Aretha (1942–), singer

Gipp, George "the Gipper" (1895–1920), football player

Johnson, Earvin "Magic" (1959–), basketball player

Leonard, Elmore (1925–), author

Lindbergh, Charles A. (1902–1974), pilot, Pulitzer Prize winner

Madonna (1958–), singer

Moore, Michael (1954–), documentary filmmaker and author

Polacco, Patricia (1944–), children's author and illustrator

Pop, Iggy (1947–), singer

Quimby, Harriet (ca. 1875–1912), 1st licensed American woman pilot

Robinson, Sugar Ray (1921–1989), boxer

Tomlin, Lily (1939–), comedic actor

Truth, Sojourner (ca. 1797–1883), abolitionist and women's rights activist

Van Allsburg, Chris (1949-), children's author and illustrator

Wonder, Stevie (1950-), singer

TO FIND OUT MORE

At the Library
Carroll, Jillian. *Aretha Franklin*. Chicago: Raintree, 2004.

Fix, Alexandra. *All around Michigan: Regions and Resources*. Chicago: Heinemann Library, 2004.

Schonberg, Marcia. *Michigan History*. Chicago: Heinemann Library, 2004.

Temple, Bob. *Henry Ford: Automobile Manufacturer and Innovator*. Chanhassen, Minn.: The Child's World, 2003.

Whelan, Gloria, and Leslie Bowman (illustrator). *Night of the Full Moon*. New York: Knopf, 1993.

On the Web
Visit our home page for lots of links about Michigan: *http://www.childsworld.com/links*

Note to Parents, Teachers, and Librarians: We routinely verify our Web links to make sure they are safe, active sites—so encourage your readers to check them out!

Places to Visit or Contact
Michigan Historical Museum
702 W. Kalamazoo Street
Lansing, MI 48909
517/373-3559
For more information about the history of Michigan

Travel Michigan
300 N. Washington Square, 2nd floor
Lansing, MI 48913
888/784-7328
For more information about traveling in Michigan

INDEX

Bye, Wolverine State.
We had a great time.
We'll come back soon!